LIFEVIEWS

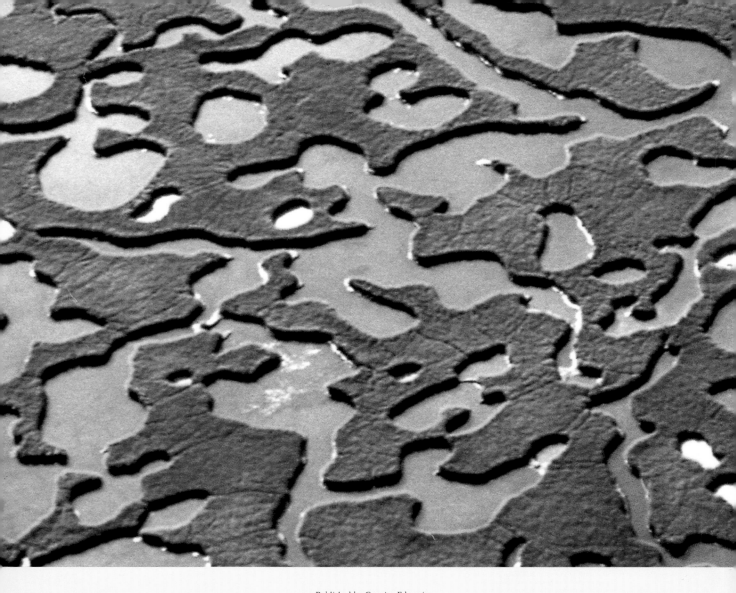

Published by Creative Education
123 South Broad Street, Mankato, Minnesota 56001
Creative Education is an imprint of The Creative Company

Art direction by Rita Marshall; Production design by The Design Lab

Photographs by Robert E. Barber, Steven Berkule, CLEO Photography, Corbis (Nathan Benn), Dennis Frates, Don Geyer, The Image Finders
(Jim Baron, Patti McConville), JLM Visuals (Richard P. Jacobs, Breck P. Kent, Lowell R. Laudon), George Robbins, Tom Stack & Associates
(Sharon Gerig, Thomas Kitchin, Brian Parker, Doug Sokell, Therisa Stack, Tom Stack, Spencer Swanger, TSADO/NASA, Greg Vaughn)

Library of Congress Cataloging-in-Publication Data

Frahm, Randy.
Rivers / by Randy Frahm.
p. cm. — (LifeViews)
Summary: Presents an overview of rivers, how they are formed, their uses, and some of the forces threatening rivers today.
ISBN 1-58341-124-0
1. Rivers—Juvenile literature. 2. Stream ecology—Juvenile literature. [1. Rivers. 2. Stream ecology. 3. Ecology.] I. Title. II. Series.
GB1203.8 .F73   2002
551.48'3—dc21   2001047901

First Edition

2 4 6 8 9 7 5 3 1

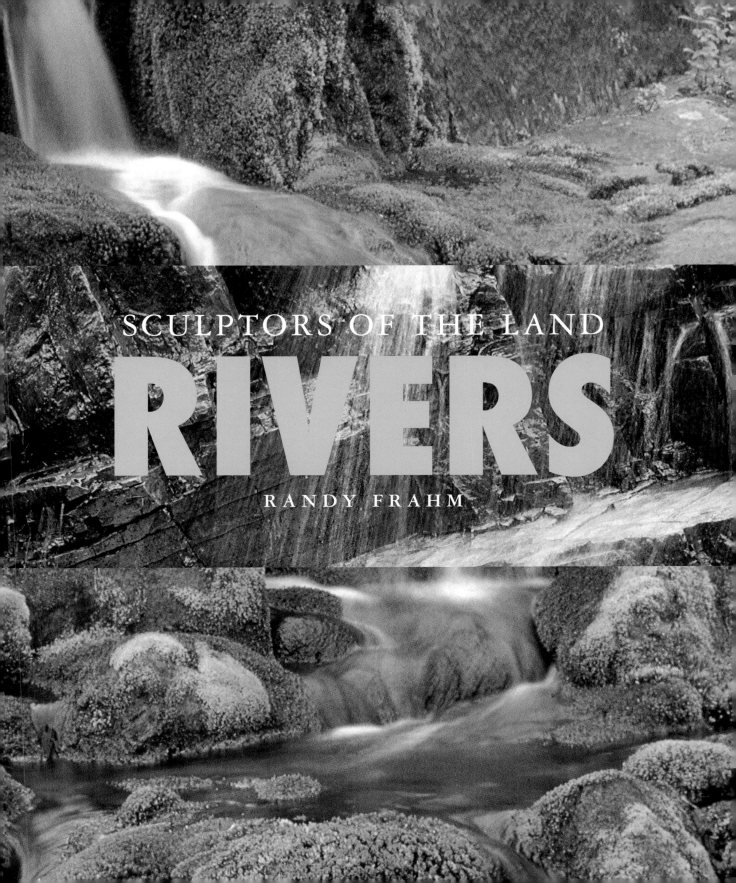

SCULPTORS OF THE LAND

RIVERS

RANDY FRAHM

CARVING AND MOLDING

the land to create astonishing works of art, rivers are nature's artists. They gouge the earth to create rocky, wide canyons that tower above churning rapids. They swell and flow over their **banks**, bringing new soil to flat, fertile floodplains. They leap off great heights to make rushing waterfalls that fill the air with **spray**.

These artists of natural change are as old as Earth itself. Rivers appeared when the rains first fell 100 billion years ago on newly formed land. Those ancient rivers were formed for the same reason modern rivers came into being: they carried excess water from land to

Rivers can dramatically change the face of the earth.

the natural storage areas of oceans and lakes. Rivers deliver a stunning amount of water—28 trillion gallons (106.4 trillion l) a day. The world's largest river is the Amazon River in South America. It carries 17 percent of the total river flow on Earth, five times more than the second-largest river, the Congo in Africa.

— The water in rivers comes from a variety of sources. A small amount comes from **precipitation**, mostly rain and snow, on the surface of the river itself. But a far greater contributor is the movement of water over land and through the ground. Rain that cannot soak into the ground feeds rivers. In mountainous regions, heavy snowfall on mountaintops melts during the spring and summer, giving birth to many rivers.

Water that flows underground provides up to a third of the flow in the world's rivers. Once water soaks into the ground, it is either used by plants or stored in the earth as **groundwater**. Groundwater often seeps into a river through its bottom, called the **riverbed**, sustaining flow during times of little precipitation. Other times, groundwater levels will be

The point at which solid water (snow or ice) changes to liquid water is called the melting point, measured at just over 32 °F (0 °C). At *exactly* 32 °F (0 °C), water can exist in both solid and liquid form.

high enough to bubble through to the surface, thus becoming a spring and the start of a river. No matter where the water comes from, over the ground or under it, the beginning of a river is called its source.

Every large river is fed by several smaller rivers, which are in turn fed by even smaller rivers. A river that feeds another one is a **tributary**. The land area drained by this system is called a river's drainage basin or **watershed**. The Mississippi River, for example, is fed by large tributaries, including the Missouri River. Farther upstream, the Missouri River takes water from smaller rivers such as the Kansas River in Kansas, the Platte River in Nebraska, and the Milk River in Montana. These are in turn fed by many smaller rivers and **creeks**. Through this system, the Mississippi River has a drainage basin of 41 percent of the mainland United States, making it the fifth-largest watershed in the world.

The course a river takes is its channel. Along any channel, there may be floodplains, valleys, canyons, waterfalls, deltas, and estuaries. Flat areas running alongside the banks are called

Much of Earth's freshwater eventually reaches the sea via a vast network of tributaries. More than 10,000 tributaries feed the Amazon River, which drains 170 billion gallons (644 billion l) of water into the Atlantic each hour.

floodplains. These are created when a river carries more water than its banks can contain. Water spills over the banks and floods the surrounding land. But when the water returns to its banks, rich soil is left behind, making floodplains highly productive—as well as highly risky—areas to farm.

Floodplains often lie at the bottom of a river valley. Valleys are usually V-shaped cuts in the earth's surface. The river itself flows through the middle of the cut. The sides of a valley can be very steep or gently sloped. Rivers make valleys early in their life, when the force of their water cuts downward to create an easy path for the river to follow. Many times, a valley will be much larger than the river it borders because the valley was formed when the river was faster and larger.

Canyons and **gorges** are basically valleys carved from stone. They are created when movement in the earth's crust thrusts a section of erodible stone upward and onto an existing river channel. The river then begins to **erode** the rock, sometimes slicing deep, long valleys into the stone in a process that can take millions of years. The Grand Canyon, created by the

For millions of years, the Colorado River has sculpted the earth on its journey from high in the Rocky Mountains to Mexico's Sea of Cortez. Great chasms, such as the Grand Canyon, testify to this river's legendary power.

Colorado River, is more than 200 miles (320 km) long, 1 mile (1.6 km) deep, and as wide as 14 miles (22 km).

In a canyon, the river channel often becomes narrower, which causes the water to run faster. The result is that many canyons hold stretches of raging, turbulent water called **rapids**. The New River Gorge in West Virginia is thought to have the greatest concentration of rapids in the United States—21 rapids in 15 miles (24 km).

Nowhere is the force of a river so dramatic as where it creates a **waterfall**. Waterfalls occur when a river channel runs off the edge of a plateau (an elevated section of land) and falls to the land below. Other times, a river runs across an area where two types of rock meet. One rock type erodes more quickly than the other, and the river eventually wears away the softer rock. The river's course falls from the stronger rock formation to the softer rock.

But no matter how strong a rock formation is, water will erode it. That's why waterfalls move upstream over time—the river will wear the top edge of a waterfall away. On the Niagara

Raging water throws droplets called spray into the air.

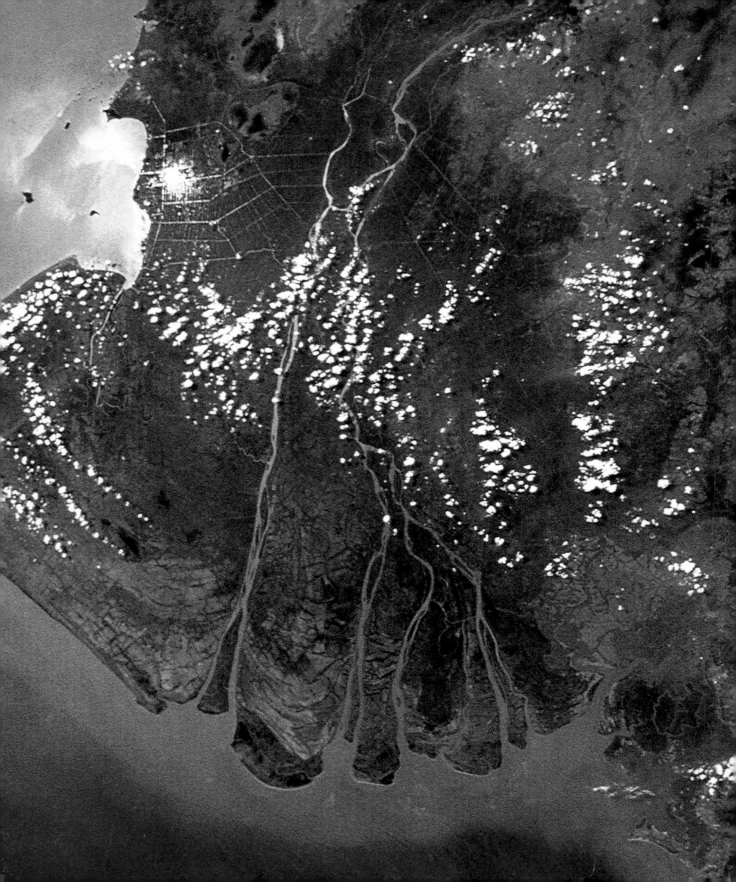

River near the U.S.-Canada border, Horseshoe Falls has moved upstream at an average rate of more than three feet (1 m) per year. The force of the water and the height from which it falls combine to make waterfalls spectacular as they fill the air with mist and thundering noise. The world's highest waterfall is Angel Falls, dropping 3,212 feet (979 m) along the Churun River in Venezuela.

Whereas waterfalls are creations of fast water, **deltas** are creations of slow water. Deltas are land masses created by rivers as they run into oceans. Rivers carry a tremendous amount of **sediment**, or particles of earth. At the point where a river reaches its destination, called its mouth, it usually widens and its current slows. As this happens, the sediment in the water settles and is shaped by both the force of the river and the waves of the ocean. Deltas take a variety of shapes. Many, like the Mississippi Delta, look like a triangle, with fingers of water spreading out from the river toward the ocean.

Estuaries are areas where the salt water of oceans mixes with the freshwater from rivers. With their unique mix of

The Mekong Delta in southern Vietnam boasts some of the world's richest agricultural land, most of which is used for rice production. Nine tributaries of the Mekong River feed the delta en route to the South China Sea.

waters, these areas provide a rich **habitat** for valuable sea life such as shrimp and crab. Because of this and the fact that estuaries provide access to both rivers and oceans, people have long been attracted to them.

The connection between humans and rivers has a long history. Some 6,000 years ago, humans made the transition from hunting and gathering food to farming. They did so along rivers, where the combination of fertile floodplain soil and plentiful river water for **irrigation** allowed for successful farming. The first civilizations developed along the floodplains of the Tigris and Euphrates rivers in what is now Iraq; along the Indus River, which runs through Pakistan; and along the Huang He (Yellow) River of China.

As civilizations grew, cities were built along rivers because the waterways allowed for the easy transportation of people and goods. Rivers also provided natural boundaries as countries were formed. For example, the Rhine River makes up part of the border between France and Germany, just as

In areas with minimal rainfall, irrigation is essential to successful farming. Crop production in the southwestern U.S. relies heavily on the Colorado River, which is used to irrigate nearly 3.5 million acres (1.4 million h) of farmland.

the Rio Grande separates Mexico and the United States.

As Europeans sailed across the oceans to North and South America, rivers in the new lands became routes of **exploration**. In the 1500s, Spanish explorers searching for riches along a South American river were attacked by women warriors from native civilizations in the area. The Spanish called these women "Amazons," after female warriors in Greek **mythology**. They also gave that name to the river they were exploring— the Amazon River. Much later, in the 1700s, Alexander Mackenzie completed a famous overland journey across North America by traveling such Canadian rivers as the Peace, Parsnip, Fraser, and Blackwater. A major river in northwest Canada carries his name today as a tribute to his achievement.

Modern societies depend on rivers as much as their predecessors did. Rivers give us water for drinking and for growing food. In ancient times, a person used between three and five gallons (11–19 l) per day. Today, the average American uses 168 gallons (638 l) daily. Ordinary activities use extraordinary amounts of water. A shower will often use between 25

Many cities around the world rely on their neighboring rivers for industrial processes, hydroelectric power, and drinking water. Therefore, care must be taken to maintain healthy river ecosystems by curbing urban waste.

and 50 gallons (95–190 l), while flushing a toilet takes five to seven gallons (19–27 l).

That sort of use can take an environmental toll. The Colorado River, which runs 1,450 miles (2,333 km) through the dry southwestern United States, supplies water to 21 million people in seven states. Water from the river is used to irrigate the majority of cropland in the area. Denver, Colorado, gets about half of its water from the river. In some areas, 90 percent of the river's flow is taken for human use. So used and reused is the Colorado River water that its flow is often reduced to a polluted trickle.

Dams have been erected along many rivers to control flooding, produce electricity, and store water for human use. But dams can alter the quality of the river water and the life in it. For example, before the Glen Canyon Dam was built on the Colorado River, water temperature varied from freezing in winter to 80 °F (27 °C) in the summer. Now water temperatures remain around 50 °F (10 °C) year-round, too cold for some of the fish native to the river, such as the humpback chub

Built responsibly, dams can be quite beneficial. The Grand Coulee Dam (top), on the Columbia River in Washington, is the third largest producer of electricity in the world, generating power for 11 western states.

and the squaw fish. **Environmentalists** advocate that such concerns be considered before planning or building new dams in the future.

Rivers are more often threatened not by the water taken out of them, but by what is put into them. **Pesticides** and fertilizer run off of farmland, while cities often dump sewage into rivers. Industrial wastes include pollutants that settle on the river bottom and remain there for years. All of these pollutants can hurt the plants and animals, including humans, that depend on the river.

Even excessive amounts of sediment can hurt a river's health. Environmentalists are concerned that the flooding along the Mississippi River in the summer of 1993 may have severely damaged **backwater** areas. Backwaters are areas of slow water away from the main flow of the river, and they provide valuable habitat for many animals and plants. The heavy rains that caused the flooding washed soil from farmland into

Diverse communities of plant and animal life live in and around rivers. From tall pine trees to mosses and algae, from fish and crustaceans to large mammals such as grizzly bears, rivers provide habitats for them all.

the river. Once in the river, the soil became sediment, or **silt**. An estimated one million tons (900,000 t) of sediment flowed past the town of Winona, Minnesota, in just five days. The danger is that this excessive sediment will settle, filling with silt much of the Upper Mississippi National Wildlife Refuge, an area that runs 260 miles (418 km) from Wabasha, Minnesota, to Rock Island, Illinois, along the Mississippi River. The silt could cause water **depths** to be reduced and thus radically alter the habitat.

As our concern for the environment grows, much attention deserves to be focused on nature's artists, the rivers. Crossing the land in intricate patterns and sustaining a vast **network** of life, rivers help shape the landscape of our planet and contribute to the quality of our lives. From source to mouth, from trickling mountain streams to triumphant outpourings to the ocean, rivers are the embodiment of natural change, history, beauty, and life itself.

From the largest to the smallest, rivers are nature's artists.

MAKING A DELTA

When a river meets the sea, its channel widens, its current slows, and all of its sediment settles, creating a land mass called a delta. Deltas were originally so named because their triangular shape resembled the Greek letter "delta." Not all deltas take on this shape, but they're still called deltas. This activity will show you how deltas form.

You Will Need

- Three boards, each about 1 x 4 x 24 inches (3 x 10 x 61 cm) long
- A small piece of scrap wood
- A hammer
- Nails
- Aluminum foil
- A large cake pan
- A mixture of sand, small rocks, pebbles, silt, and clay
- A wood block or other prop, such as a book
- A watering can full of water

Constructing the "Mouth"

1. Nail the three boards together to form a trough. Nail the piece of scrap wood to one end to close it off. This trough will be your river channel.

2. Line the inside of the trough with aluminum foil to waterproof it.

3. Fill the trough about half full with the sand and rock mixture. This mixture simulates the sediment at the bottom of a river.

4. Set the open end of the trough on one end of the cake pan (the "ocean") and prop the closed end up at a slight angle with the wood block.

5. Slowly pour the water onto the raised end of the trough, the "head" of your river. As the water flows over the sand and rocks, particles will be picked up and carried to the lowered end of the trough, the "mouth" of your river.

Observation

Notice how the heaviest particles, the small rocks and pebbles, settle first, closest to the river's mouth. As the water fans out into the ocean, a triangular-shaped mass of sediment starts to form. The lighter the sediment is, the farther out it will be carried. Fine particles such as silt and clay will travel farthest.

Deltas are usually very fertile lands because of the nutrients contained in the sediment. As a result, a variety of plant and animal life make their homes there. Many of the world's largest rivers form deltas, including the Nile, Rhine, Danube, Tigris, and Huang He (Yellow). The Mississippi River, which runs from northern Minnesota to Louisiana, makes about 200 feet (60 m) of delta in the Gulf of Mexico each year.

STAYING AFLOAT

How do boats, especially large ones such as barges, stay afloat? It would seem that the larger a boat is, the more likely it would be to sink. But this isn't so. The more area an object covers, the better it floats. You can test this theory for yourself with a bowl of water and some aluminum foil.

First, fill a large bowl with water. Cut two pieces of aluminum foil, each about three by six inches (8 x 13 cm). Crumple one piece into a very loose wad and set it on top of the water. It floats! Next, roll the other piece into the tightest, smallest ball you can. Set the ball on the water. It sinks!

Water pushes up against objects on its surface. This lifting force causes objects to float. Even though both pieces of foil were the same size and weight, the loose wad covered a larger area of water; therefore, there was more water to "lift" it. The compacted ball took up a much smaller area of water and had less water to support it, so it sank. This explains how huge steel ships stay afloat. They spread their weight out across a large area. If they were compacted like the ball, they too would sink. An object's ability to float is referred to as its buoyancy. An object that floats well is said to be buoyant.

LEARN MORE ABOUT RIVERS

American Rivers
1025 Vermont Avenue NW
Suite 720
Washington, D.C. 20005
http://www.amrivers.org

Environment Canada:
    The Sturgeon General Reports
(online ecology discussion of the Fraser
    River watershed)
http://www.sturgeongeneral.org

International Rivers Network
1847 Berkeley Way
Berkeley, CA 94703
http://www.irn.org

U.S. Environmental Protection Agency
Mail Code 4503F
401 M Street SW
Washington, D.C. 20460
http://www.epa.gov/iwi

U.S. Fish and Wildlife Service
(offices in every state; check the website
    or your local telephone directory for
    listings)
http://www.fws.gov

World Wildlife Fund
1250 24th Street NW
Washington, D.C. 20037
http://www.worldwildlife.org/amazon

INDEX

Directly or indirectly, rivers feed all life on Earth.